A

VOICE

A

VISION

A

VICTORY

GARTH COONCE

A VOICE, A VISION, A VICTORY

Copyright © 2010 by Garth Coonce

ISBN: 0-9777813-4-8

Published by
TCT MINISTRIES, INC.
P.O BOX 1010
MARION, IL 62959

Printed in the United States of America.

DEDICATION

*This book is dedicated to my
wife, Tina, for her love, support, and
total dedication to our family
and the ministry.*

CONTENTS

INTRODUCTION

Recently, TCT began broadcasting on our newest television station, WRAY-TV, channel 42, serving Raleigh, Durham, Chapel Hill, and Fayetteville, North Carolina. It is our 18th over-the-air facility and we are thrilled with the response we are receiving from this area.

I have often been asked, "Why would you want to expand during such tough economic times? Does it really make sense?"

If you listen to the secular media, the future is filled with peril, but during the past three decades, I have learned a valuable lesson. When God gives you a word that says, "Go," it's not the time to hesitate. Just the opposite. It's the hour to move forward.

In fact, it is when the world's economy is in a downturn that God's Kingdom soars to new heights. As I look back on the milestones of our ministry, many of the TCT stations that now broadcast the Gospel 24 hours a day were purchased at far below market prices because the previous owners were near bankruptcy and were anxious for someone to bail them out.

As you will discover in this book, even before we launched this ministry, it was the unmistakable voice of the Lord that gave me direction. And today, He is still speaking. As I write these words, God is impressing this Scripture on my heart: *"I will never leave you nor forsake you"* (Hebrews 13:5).

Regardless of the crisis that may be swirling around you during these uncertain times, *"This hope we have as an anchor of the soul, both secure and steadfast"* (Hebrews 6:19).

WHOSE VOICE WILL YOU HEAR?

This book was written to help you learn how to hear the voice of the Lord. And if you will obey His words, He will reveal the vision He has for your future. These are the necessary steps that will lead you to amazing triumphs and victories God has planned—just for you.

——— *v* ———
This book was written to help you learn how to hear the voice of the Lord.

On these pages we will look at

the story of Creation in a fresh light. Adam and Eve had the world at their command, and God gave them simple, yet clear, rules to live by. But instead, they listened to Satan who came in the form of a serpent. He told them the world's greatest lie. Rather than feasting their eyes —and their tastebuds—on the Lord's unlimited abundance, they chose to look in a deadly direction.

_____ *V* _____

The result of their decision changed the course of history and impacts your life today.

The result of their decision changed the course of history and impacts your life today.

As a successful businessman, I also heard two voices. The Lord, in words that were unmistakable, told me specifically what He wanted me to do. At the same time, Satan was up to his schemes, filling my mind with doubt.

You will learn that the decision I made has resulted in bringing the Gospel to millions of people through Total Christian Television.

During these years of ministry, I have seen firsthand what happens when people lose their spiritual hearing. Some of our close friends, who shared the excitement and joy of the early days of this adventure, suddenly lost the vision of where God was leading. Their commitment turned to complaining. Their joy turned to jealousy and bitterness. It happened when they began to look in the wrong direction. To this day, Tina and I ache for the loss of those friends.

"PLANS TO PROSPER"

The Lord has an exciting plan to restore your ability to hear His voice. The tragedy of the tree in the Garden resulted in the triumph at the tree of Calvary. Jesus is alive! He is ready at this very moment to help you refocus on God's vision for your life so you will begin to clearly see His love, His grace, and His forgiveness. Even more, you will *experience* it!

The tragedy of the tree in the Garden resulted in the triumph at the tree of Calvary. Jesus is alive!

The words the Lord spoke to the prophet Jeremiah are true for you today: *"For I know the plans I have for you...plans to prosper you and not to harm you, plans to give you hope and a future"* (Jeremiah 29:11 NIV).

10

Thanks for joining me on this journey. It is my prayer that you will not only hear God's voice and receive His vision, but experience the victory He has prepared especially for you.

— *Garth Coonce*

CHAPTER ONE

DON'T IGNORE
THE INSTRUCTIONS

Listen to counsel and receive instruction,
that you may be wise in your latter days.
– PROVERBS 19:20

The first time I looked through the lens of a television camera, I had no earthly idea that one day, the Lord would use me to send the voice and vision of the Gospel to millions of homes in the United States. Around the world, in Europe, Asia, the Middle East, Africa, India, and the Philippines, potentially 1.5 billion viewers receive the TCT signal from their television stations via global satellites as well as direct-to-home and cable stations.

Even before I heard the voice of the Lord give me direction for my future, God was preparing me for what was ahead.

EXCITED, NERVOUS, AND PETRIFIED!

I can still remember when I was twelve years old and had thoughts of a different kind. I was dreaming of going hunting but no one had ever taught me how to shoot. I'd played cops and robbers, yet had never held a real shotgun in my hand.

This all changed when my Uncle Basil came over to our house with his single-shot, 12-gauge shotgun. We went out in the backyard and set up a few empty Campbell soup cans.

At the moment my uncle handed me the gun, I was excited, nervous, and petrified all at the same time. The weapon seemed almost as heavy as I was!

These were his instructions: "Keep your eyes wide open and look right down the barrel at one of those cans." Then he added, "If you're ever going to get a rabbit or a pheasant, you need to learn how to focus. You've got to have accurate aim."

That particular weapon had a lever on it that you cocked. He showed me exactly how it worked and warned, "Be mighty careful, Garth, because as soon as you touch that trigger it will fire."

PULLING THE TRIGGER

I followed his instructions and spread my legs apart, keeping them as stiff as a board. He told me to look down the barrel, but excitement got the better of me and my eyes didn't seem to go in the same direction. I couldn't see beyond the end of the gun.

It took a little while before I was able to get that enormous shotgun aimed, and finally I saw the cans out there.

If I live to be 120 I will never forget the first time I pulled that trigger.

"Bam!" I thought it was going to take my arm right off. The pain I suddenly felt in the palm of my hand was unbearable.

—— V ——

If I live to be 120 I will never forget the first time I pulled that trigger.

The powerful recoil had jammed the lever so deep into my hand it began to bleed. To this day I still bear the scar.

Undeterred, Uncle Basil said, "Put in another shot and try it again. And remember, focus on that can."

I did my best to be strong and brave, but by now I was not only considering focusing or aiming. I was considering life itself!

"This thing is going to kill me for sure," I thought as I felt my aching shoulder and throbbing hand.

"BUCK FEVER"

Several days later Uncle Basil announced, "Garth, I think it's time you get out in the field and shoot some real game."

As we walked through those tall grasses with that shotgun my only thoughts were: "I sure hope nothing takes off—running or flying. What if a rabbit jumps out? What if a pheasant appears? What am I going to do?"

——*v*——
"I sure hope nothing takes off—running or flying."

After awhile I finally spotted a rabbit, but was overcome with what they call "buck fever." I pulled the trigger before the shotgun ever got to my arm. As you can imagine, the shot went one way and the rabbit ran the other.

During those days as a fledgling hunter, I had much more to remember about handling a gun than merely focusing. But the more I practiced, the easier it became. Finally the day arrived when I could put all the pieces together. "Ready, aim, fire!" became more than an uncoordinated three-step process and I was able to bring home a good trophy.

At that time in my young life I had no idea what the future would hold. How could I know that God would give me something far greater at which to aim? How could I foresee that He would call me to focus on *His* vision? How could I anticipate that someday, instead of looking through the scope of a weapon, I would be aiming the message of Christ to millions of men, women, and children?

WHAT A GARDEN!

Let me tell you about another man who heard a voice and received instructions regarding how he was to live.

Long before you and I were born, God created an exquisite, beautiful world. In His infinite wisdom, He created man and placed him in a Garden called Eden. *"The Lord God planted a garden eastward in Eden, and there He put the man whom He had formed"* (Genesis 2:8).

17

What a glorious place of splendor. It was beyond description. *"And the Lord God made all kinds of trees grow out of the ground—trees that were pleasing to the eye and good for food"* (verse 9 NIV).

In our travels, Tina and I have been privileged to see the flowering cherry blossom trees of Washington, D.C., the lush landscape of Cypress Gardens, Florida, and famous gardens of Europe and the Orient, but I believe they cannot compare to what God created in Eden.

TWO UNUSUAL TREES

No matter where he looked, Adam saw beauty— untold numbers of gorgeous trees and flowers, and delicious fruit hanging from the branches. It was a "luscious" Garden that was both gorgeous and flawless. He must have been overwhelmed by so many wonderful sights.

However, growing right in the middle of Eden were two unusual trees. Scripture tells us, *"The tree of life was also in the midst of the garden, and the tree of the knowledge of good and evil"* (verse 9).

The Lord gave Adam specific orders regarding his

responsibilities. He was to look after the Garden and preserve its beauty. *"Then the Lord God took the man and put him in the garden of Eden to tend and keep it"* (verse 15).

The Almighty also gave Adam a great lesson concerning the focus of his life. He told him what he could eat—and what he couldn't. *"Of every tree of the garden you may freely eat; but of the tree of the knowledge of good and evil you shall not eat, for in the day that you eat of it you shall surely die"* (Genesis 2:16-17).

—— V ——

The Almighty gave Adam a great lesson concerning the focus of his life.

A DIRECT WARNING

Adam had complete freedom to enjoy the fruit of countless trees in the Garden. He had free reign of Eden. All God desired was that he not touch the one tree in the center.

The Creator was saying, "Listen to Me. All I am asking is that you stay away from the Tree of Good and Evil. The rest is yours. If you obey Me, I will walk by your side and provide for all of your needs."

However, there was a clear warning: "Don't eat from that one tree. It will kill and destroy you." This was not a casual suggestion, but a command of Almighty God. The Lord didn't imply, "It would be nice if you did these things." Instead, it was a direct order. The Bible tells us the Lord "commanded" Adam. God decreed that if man ate of that one tree, "you shall surely die."

> —— *ν* ——
> *God decreed that if man ate of that one tree, "you shall surely die."*

GUIDELINES FOR LIFE

I'm sure you have heard the phrase that "God is a God of abundance." No one knew this truth better than Adam. He was surrounded with good things to eat. There was beauty as far as the eye could see.

Not long after God gave Adam his instructions, He also gave him a companion. *"And the Lord God said, 'It is not good that man should be alone; I will make him a helper comparable to him'"* (Genesis 2:18).

She was given the name Eve—meaning "the life-giving one."

The first man, Adam, shared God's guidelines with his wife as they began life's journey together. There was so much they could enjoy—and so little they could not.

The Wrong Voice

What took place next was something they were not prepared for—Satan, appeared in the form of a snake. *"Now the serpent was more cunning than any beast of the field which the Lord God had made. And he said to the woman, 'Has God indeed said, "You shall not eat of every tree of the garden?"'* (Genesis 3:1).

Responding to the serpent's question, Eve replied, *"We may eat the fruit of the trees of the garden; but of the fruit of the tree which is in the midst of the garden, God has said, 'You shall not eat it, nor shall you touch it, lest you die'"* (verses 2-3).

Next, Satan told Eve his big lie. *"And the serpent said to the woman, 'You will not surely die. For God knows that in the day you eat of it your eyes will be opened, and you will be like God, knowing good and evil'"* (verses 4-5).

The devil's cunning message worked. *"So when the woman saw that the tree was good for food, that it was pleasant to the eyes, and a tree desirable to make one wise, she took of its fruit and ate. She also gave to her husband with her, and he ate"* (verse 6).

From that moment, Eve began to focus on that one tree and disregarded the voice of God and what was truly in her best interest. It was as though she became blinded to everything else in Eden.

Rather than looking at the abundant alternatives, her eyes were riveted on the one tree that was the object of God's warning, and she was taken in by the devil's deceit.

Her gaze turned from looking to God and His creation to looking at sin. It was as if a magnet were pulling her toward the object they were not to touch. What she failed to realize was that you cannot look at God and sin at the same time. They are not compatible.

THE CUNNING DECEIVER

It must have broken the heart of the Almighty to see Eve partake of the forbidden fruit; she offered some to her husband and he also ate. Adam joined her in disobedience to God and the fall of man occurred—sin entered the world. It was at that precise moment Satan began his quest to destroy mankind.

Even today, millions—including God-fearing Christians—fail to realize the seduction of Satan. They proclaim, "I've got power over the devil in the name of Jesus. He can't touch me."

While this is true and we should ultimately believe and act upon it, we should never forget the deceptive manner in which the devil operates. The Bible says, *"The serpent was more cunning than any beast of the field which the Lord God had made"* (Genesis 3:1).

THE BATTLE OF GOOD AND EVIL

Be warned! There are times when Satan shrewdly enters the arena of our life and we are almost unaware of what has happened. It isn't because there is less power in the name of Jesus—His name is still all-powerful and the devil will flee from it. But when we allow our eyes to wander from the Lord and look elsewhere, we begin to lose our protection.

When we allow our eyes to wander from the Lord and look elsewhere, we begin to lose our protection.

This is exactly what happened to the keepers of the

Garden. The moment they ate of the only tree they were warned to avoid, Adam and Eve began the struggle of sin—the battle of right and wrong, good and evil. *"Then the eyes of both of them were opened, and they knew that they were naked; and they sewed fig leaves together and made themselves coverings"* (Genesis 3:7).

How tragic! If only they had paused for a moment to consider God's command. If only they had been a mile away from the serpent enjoying the pleasures of the Garden, the snake could have hung in that tree all day without attracting their attention. They would not have eaten the fatal fruit.

THE BIG LIE

Adam and Eve wandered far too close to Satan, and this reminds me of so many people today.

I can picture them approaching the succulent fruit and rationalizing, "Well, we're not supposed to eat it, but surely there won't be any harm in touching."

As they were about to caress the fruit, they probably said, "Let's see what it feels like. I wonder what it smells like?"

At that point, they were so near that Satan could dangle from a branch and whisper, "Go ahead! It won't hurt you."

Well, it obviously didn't take much persuasion because Adam and Eve wanted to do things their own way. God took second place and they became partakers of sin.

As a direct result of their actions, the Lord placed a curse on Adam and Eve and they were banished from the Garden.

Thousands of years later, we still are faced with the same choice as God's original creation. Yet, some would tell you, "If that had been me in the Garden, I wouldn't have been so foolish to have fallen for Satan's trick, and the world would be a different place."

> *We are falling for the devil's deceptions minute by minute.*

Such an argument doesn't hold water. My friend, we are falling for the devil's deceptions minute by minute. I believe it doesn't require as much of a ploy today as it did back then. Satan doesn't offer just one temptation, but *thousands!*

25

A Deadly Shift of Attention

In the Garden, God told them, "Everything is yours. You can do absolutely anything you want with this fruit. Eat and enjoy! It will keep you healthy, joyful, will lift your spirits, and provide life itself. But remember, you must not touch the tree in the center."

As we read the account in Genesis, it seems that Adam and Eve, instead of listening to the Lord and delighting in their environment, became completely engrossed in the one thing they couldn't have. What consumed them was the forbidden fruit.

Sadly, it didn't take much effort for Satan to entice the first man and woman because their attention was already turned away from God.

This is still happening. We know from Scripture that there are certain things that will bring condemnation on us if we willfully do them. Yet, we slowly begin to shift our attention from the goodness of God to the evils of the enemy. Before we realize what has happened, our eyes begin to zero in on the things that would destroy us.

The Creator wants you to hear His voice and receive a new, clear vision of the great future He sees for your life. He not only wants to inspire you, but wants you to aim for the dream He has planned—*the purpose for which you were placed on this earth.*

Thankfully, the Lord has an unending supply of peace, joy, and blessing in store.

When you place these on the balance scale of life, His good pleasures vastly outweigh the few items God has asked you to avoid.

What Does the Lord Want?

The sound advice I received from Uncle Basil at the age of twelve is still relevant today. If I listened carefully to his instruction, had a clear objective, and looked straight down the barrel, I was going to hit the target. But first, I had to learn to look beyond the end of the shotgun. I had to focus on what God wanted for my life—not what Satan desired, or even what I hoped for.

This was a lesson I would certainly need.

CHAPTER TWO

"WHOSE VOICE WAS SPEAKING?"

I heard the voice of the Lord, saying:
"Whom shall I send, And who will go for Us?" Then
I said, "Here am I! Send me."

— ISAIAH 6:8

I will never forget Thanksgiving, 1976.

There was plenty to thank God for. I had a wonderful wife and family. I was a successful businessman with a background in management, finance, and accounting. The focus of my life was in being the best I could be—and retiring at the age of 55.

On that day, however, I heard a voice as clearly as someone standing next to me. The words were spoken calmly, but with great and unmistakable force: "I want you to build a Christian television station in Cincinnati."

Since I was not prone to hearing "voices" and

nothing like this had ever happened to me before, I didn't tell anyone about what I had heard. In fact, I tried to shrug off the experience and forget it had ever occurred.

Two months later, it happened again. It was the same voice, and the same message: "I want you to build a Christian television station in Cincinnati."

"Who was this?" I wondered. "Is God really trying to talk to me?"

Next, I questioned, "Why me?" And I thought, "Christian television?" I knew absolutely nothing about TV except how to turn on my set and click through the channels.

> ——V——
> "Who was this?" I wondered. "Is God really trying to talk to me?"

I decided it was time to share with Tina what God was telling me.

Her words were more than encouraging. "Garth, if this is what the Lord wants us to do, I'm with you one hundred percent." From that moment we made it a top priority in our prayer life. We needed to know God's will.

A VOICE FROM HEAVEN

When you begin to study Scripture, you discover

that again and again the Lord speaks to His people. His powerful voice comes in many forms:

- As the sound of harps (Isaiah 30:31-32; Revelation 14:2).
- As the sound of many waters (Ezekiel 43:2; Revelation 1:15; 14:2).
- As the sound of trumpets (Exodus 19:16,19; Hebrews 12:19).
- As the sound of thunder (Job 40:9; Psalm 29:3).

God speaks directly to man—just as He did to Adam and Eve (Genesis 3:8), Abraham (Genesis 12:1-3), Moses (Exodus 3:4), Elijah (1 Kings 19:9) and so many more. Even Peter, James, and John heard God's voice say, *"This is My beloved Son, in whom I am well pleased. Hear Him!"* (Matthew 17:5).

Yes, the Almighty speaks audibly, and allows us to personally hear from heaven.

"WE'RE READY TO HELP"

A short time later, in the spring of 1977, Tina and

31

I were involved with our church in leading "Life in the Spirit" seminars, and at the closing night of a series, Pastor Clyde Miller was the guest speaker. After the seminar, Tina and I, along with several couples, were talking with Pastor Miller.

Suddenly, for the first time I felt the urge to share what had been stirring deep in my heart. "The Lord has been speaking to me since last Thanksgiving to build a Christian television station to cover this area with the Gospel," I told them. "I just can't get it out of my spirit."

> *"Let's go for it! We've never attempted anything like this before."*

A friend named Chuck Payne, who was standing there with his wife, Myra, said, "If that is what the Lord wants, we're ready to help." Someone else spoke up, "Let's go for it! We've never attempted anything like this before."

To my amazement, the group became alive with the possibilities of where God was leading. Then, like a blanket descending from heaven, a spirit of prayer came over us. We joined hands together and began to pray fervently.

A "High Mountain"

During that special time of prayer, the Lord revealed Himself to us through a Scripture: *"Get up into the high mountain; O Jerusalem, you who bring good tidings, lift up your voice with strength, lift it up, be not afraid: say to the cities... 'Behold your God!'"* (Isaiah 40:9).

It was as if the Lord Himself had spoken, and those words encouraged us to go forward even though we had no idea of the obstacles we were about to face. But that was a blessing in disguise since we couldn't look to ourselves for strength. We had to look to the Lord.

Only One Problem

Not long after, Chuck, who was in the banking business, talked with one of his lawyer friends and we had our first donation—the legal papers to form a corporation. Immediately, we organized a board of directors and a small team of people who believed the Lord had a great work for us to do.

However, there was only one problem; none of us

knew anything about building a television station! Bryan Perkins was selling electrical equipment. Bob Stein was with IBM in management. Jim Whittington was a chemical engineer.

Chuck Payne opened a small post office box close to where he worked so he could make the deposits of the checks we prayed would be coming in.

I smile when I think of the first "office" for the ministry. It was a Frisch's Big Boy restaurant located half way between where Chuck and I worked. We were on opposite sides of the city.

One day the phone rang. "Garth. You'll never believe it!" exclaimed Chuck. "I've just made our first deposit. We received a check for $10." "Praise God," we both said. You'd have thought it was a million!

DEAD SILENCE!

The first telephone call I made to the Federal Communications Commission was a real learning experience. When I was connected to a man in the television division, I spoke right to the point: "We want to build a Christian television station in Cincinnati. How do we get a license?"

Obviously, I was a novice. There was dead silence for a while and then I heard a chuckle. The fellow said, "It's not possible! There are no allocations for Cincinnati and this isn't the way you do it."

____ V ____

"It's not possible!"

The gentleman began to tell me about the necessity for engineering studies, financial records, competitive FCC hearings, etc., and I asked him, "Just send me any information you have."

However, there was one thing I *did* know. The Lord had clearly spoken that we were to build a Christian station and I was determined to keep my eye on that goal.

My next step was to visit a friend who was a realtor and I told him, "We need a 40-acre piece of property on which to build a television tower."

He asked, "Where do you want me to look?"

Pointing to a precise spot on the map, I responded, "Right there." The Lord had shown me that from that location the signal would reach Dayton, Cincinnati, and Richmond, Indiana.

Trying to be of help, he said, "Let me see what I can do."

A HIGH TOWER

Only one day later, the realtor came back with a listing on a piece of property exactly where the Lord showed us we should be. When we received the topography survey we were amazed to learn that it was the highest point in the whole area.

I knew this was an answer to prayer. Surely this was the "mountain" from which the Word of the Lord would be powerfully proclaimed.

——— *v* ———
Money was a big problem —we didn't have any!

Money was a big problem—we didn't have any! But we did put an option on the land since we knew that is where the tower must be built. However, first we would need the approval of both the FCC and the Federal Aviation Administration—they don't want aircraft bumping into strange towers.

SPREADING THE WORD

Starting that very week, we began to speak anywhere we could about the vision God had placed in our hearts. Big meetings, little meetings, prayer groups, Sunday School classes—*it didn't matter.*

In a rush to spread the word, we scheduled dinners, banquets, and rallies to tell the story of God's leading. On Sunday morning, Sunday night, and Wednesday night, we would drive to churches who would give us a few minutes—and sometimes the entire service—to share the possibilities.

We had no idea what the response would be. And it was as varied as anything we could have imagined.

One concerned woman said, "You're going to build a *what?"*

A gentleman asked, "Why do we need Christian television?"

Many others responded, "We're praying for you."

I wish I could tell you there was a great outpouring of financial support, but that wasn't the case. We literally had to pray in the funds day after day to see the project inch slowly forward.

The luxury of a "full time" staff didn't exist. We all continued in our occupations and dedicated every moment of our spare time to seeing the vision fulfilled. To help people "see" the project, we took along some visual aids, including a big map to show exactly where the tower would beam out the message.

OUR "EQUIPMENT"

I vividly remember what I call a "red letter" day. It was when we were able to get our first television camera—a Sony. We opened the box on our kitchen table and didn't have the slightest idea how it worked or what to do with it. Several of us were intently pouring over the instruction manual trying to put it together. It took nearly three days.

Since we were so anxious to show people how Christian television was actually going to look, we obtained two used cameras from a local university and began to set all three of them up in our meetings for a demonstration.

——— *V* ———
Chuck— the banker —became our director and engineer.

Meeting after meeting, day after day, we would haul the new equipment from our basement to a presentation—then back again. *Oh, it was heavy!*

In addition to our cameras and monitors, we showed clips of some of the programs we would be bringing to the area. Chuck—the banker—became our director and "engineer."

Early "Productions"

I remember Steve Brock, who now sings on many national television programs. He was pastoring a local church and we set up our cameras there for a service. We attempted to make a video tape. That was the night the image on one unit turned out to be green, and the picture from another camera was totally red —and the third was somewhere in the middle. Even then our problem was focus—the cameras wouldn't always cooperate and we didn't know how to solve the problem. This is how we introduced Steve Brock to Christian television!

A short time later we met some believers in the television advertising department of the Proctor and Gamble corporation. They volunteered to help us with our church "productions," which greatly enhanced our ability to communicate. One of the men became an executive of the Christian Broadcasting Network in Virginia Beach, Virginia.

Miraculous Confirmations

Forget about perfection. We were just a handful of

people trying to follow God's leading the best we knew how. Just ordinary men and women working at regular jobs, not seeking to be in full-time ministry. But somehow God linked us all together to form a spiritual network before He would establish an electronic one.

I wish you could have attended our pot luck dinners. They would turn into dynamic prayer and praise meetings as the Lord would confirm His Word in miraculous ways. As time progressed, hundreds of people from many churches became involved in the project—from intercessory prayer to faithfully putting out newsletters.

HOW COULD THIS HAPPEN?

One day, to my great surprise, I received a shocking telephone call. It was from the real estate company concerning our land.

The agent said, "Garth, I think we've got a problem."

"What is it?" I asked.

"I don't know how it happened, but somehow the date for the renewal of our option expired and the paperwork was not refiled. The farmer has accepted an offer from some other people who are going to build a house on the property."

My heart literally sank. I couldn't believe it! How could something like this happen? Didn't God tell me we were going to have that property?

The official application we presented to the FCC and the FAA was based on that particular site. If we didn't have it we would have to start all over. During those years it was extremely difficult to get the approval for a new station.

Feeling sick to my stomach, I dropped to my knees and prayed, "Lord, what is happening? I need to hear from You."

CHAPTER THREE

THE SOUND OF THE SHEPHERD

My sheep hear My voice, and
I know them, and they follow Me.
– JOHN 10:27

Looking back, the Lord didn't promise that the road would be easy, He only told us to keep our eyes fixed on Him. I thought this was what we had done, so why had we lost the option on our land? I just couldn't understand.

It didn't take long for me to realize that when you invade Satan's territory you'd better be prepared for spiritual warfare. Christian broadcasting is an all-out attack on the devil because when the signal begins to vibrate through the airwaves, it literally shakes up his kingdom. After all, he claims to be the "Prince of the power of the air."

However, this is a struggle we should welcome because it can cause us to grow and mature in the body of Christ. We become seasoned soldiers in the battle—winning victory after victory in the Name of the Lord.

INTENSE WARFARE

In Cincinnati, there were times I felt we were like the Children of Israel in the wilderness, confronting one obstacle after another. With an objective to cover a city with the Gospel of Christ, we should not have been surprised at Satan's resistance. The battle became intense.

At that point in my life, I had lived for the Lord and studied His Word for years. I felt I was ready to handle anything the devil could throw my way. But when you step one foot into Christian broadcasting, you realize how little you really understand about the ugly force of Satan. We experienced it firsthand—and some of the events were painful.

The situation was hard to cope with. We were only <u>one day</u> past the option renewal date and the farmer sold the land. To say this was a time of intense prayer is an understatement.

A PROPHETIC WORD

In less than thirty days we received a call from the farmer. "Would you like to renew your option?" he asked.

I was shocked. This was music to my ears. "What happened?" I wanted to know.

"Well, the man who was going to buy it couldn't come up with the financing and had to back out of the deal. It is yours if you want it!"

At that moment, I knew God was at work. We drove as fast as we could to sign the papers.

I was shocked. This was music to my ears. "What happened? I wanted to know."

Evangelist Dick Mills was in a meeting with us and we rejoiced together as I shared the good news.

God gave Mills what I believe was a prophetic word—just for Tina and me. He spoke: *"I will put a stop gap on the loss of your time, money, and energy and I will rebuke the devourer for your sake. You shall be satisfied with favor and full of the blessing of the Lord. You will have sufficient strength to meet the needs of every day. I will give you my rest."*

The evangelist continued: *"I will deliver you from the bondage of constant struggling to attain goals and you will have freedom to enjoy and relax in green pastures beside quiet waters. Your mouth will be filled with laughter and singing. Your neighbors will see what I have done for you. You will be blessed as you sow beside all water. There are people who need you, therefore I will bless you and you will minister to them."*

We humbly received this because God's Word tells us, *"Neglect not the gift that is in thee, which was given thee by prophesy"* (1 Timothy 4:14).

TOSSING AND TURNING

At this time, the FCC had not yet granted our license, but with total confidence in God, we felt the need to dedicate the transmitter tower site to the Lord. We invited every volunteer who had helped us to come out to the land for a picnic and a special service on July 4, 1978.

To us, this was an act of simple faith. We believed with all our hearts the station would be built on that property and it would beam out the Gospel 24 hours a day.

I was tossing and turning the night before the dedication rally. "Lord," I cried, "I need to hear from You before we take this important step. Please give me some direction."

"Lord," I cried. "I need to hear from You before we take this important step."

For nearly two years we had been working on the project and I was still struggling with how we were going to fill 24 hours of air time every day. "Who is going to watch?" I worried. "What kinds of programs are we going to air? Will people really be drawn to our message?"

FRIGHTENING THOUGHTS

As part of the process, we had talked to a couple of large Christian ministries and viewed the videotapes of what was being produced around the country. But when you think about filling 168 hours a week with programming people will actually sit down in their living rooms and watch—the very thought was intimidating.

I could still remember the early days of black and white television with Bishop Fulton Sheen standing in front of a curtain, just talking to the camera. I wondered, "Is that what we will be doing?" I could envision such a production and I thought, "Nobody, including me, is going to watch."

In the midnight hours I was calling out to God, "Before we dedicate this land, I need a glimpse of what is going to happen when we start sending out a signal."

> *"Before we dedicate this land, I need a glimpse of what is going to happen when we start sending out a signal."*

I knew we were obeying God's direction, but still did not have the complete picture of what it could accomplish.

HE WILL SEARCH OUT HIS SHEEP

Before the sun came up, I reached for my Bible and it fell open to the Book of Ezekiel. As I began to read, suddenly the words seemed to lift right off the page. There it was! God was putting my mind to rest as to what Christian television could be.

These were the words I read: *"For thus says the Lord God: 'Indeed I Myself will search for My sheep and seek them out"* (Ezekiel 34:11). The Living Bible says, *"I will both search and find my sheep."*

God distinctly told me, "You put the message out and I will find My sheep. You won't have to worry who is watching, or where. You won't have to be concerned about where the signal is reaching. Just be obedient and I will both search and find My sheep."

——— *V* ———

"Just be obedient and I will both search and find My sheep."

The Scripture continued, *"As a shepherd seeks out his flock on the day he is among his scattered sheep, so will I seek out My sheep and deliver them from all the places where they were scattered on a cloudy and dark day...I will feed them in good pasture, and their fold shall be on the high mountains...I will seek what was lost and bring back what was driven away, bind up the broken and strengthen what was sick"* (Ezekiel 34:12,14,16).

The message was unavoidable. God was telling me, "I will seek them out." I no longer had to worry about who would be reached. He only asked me to be faithful in delivering the Word.

SHOWERS OF LIGHTNING!

As only the Almighty could, He was showing me the dynamic potential of what would occur on the 40 acres of overgrown pasture land. I could visualize the 1,000 foot tower rising out of the ground in the middle of the property. From the top of the tower I saw the antenna spraying out beams of light in every direction. It was like a giant fireworks display; showers of lightning, filling the airwaves with glowing flames of fire.

——*V*——

I could visualize the 1,000 foot tower rising out of the ground in the middle of the property.

In that moment I knew what it meant when God said, *"I will make...the places all around My hill a blessing; and I will cause showers to come down in their season; there shall be showers of blessing"* (Ezekiel 34:26).

50

This was a vivid vision. The full power of the signal was spraying huge sparks that were landing everywhere. With every spark, the power of the Gospel was coming alive—touching people with the message of Jesus.

——— *V* ———
The full power of the signal was spraying huge sparks that were landing everywhere.

Then God revealed, "That is my Gospel going forth. I am searching out My sheep."

"They shall be safe in their land; and they shall know that I am the Lord, when I have broken the bands of their yoke and delivered them from the hand of those who enslaved them" (verse 27).

GOD'S FIREWORKS!

I was anxious to drive to the tower site that morning. When we arrived, there was a large crowd already gathering and we had a glorious day of dedication.

Out in the field, I shared what God had revealed, telling them, "If we simply send the signal out, He will do the rest. He will search out His sheep."

I also told them of my vision of a giant tower that would shower the entire broadcast area with flames of the Gospel message. It was the Fourth of July and the sun was shining brightly, but by faith we could see God's fireworks!

In our culture, we have been conditioned for generations to believe that in order to minister to the lost you have to physically "see" them—in a church or a meeting hall. Through the medium of television, however, you don't have the faintest idea who is watching, or exactly how they are being reached. We were entering into a ministry that would cause us to rely totally on the Holy Spirit to touch the hearts of people.

From the day we dedicated the land, it took three more years of diligent work—of peaks and valleys—of disappointments and great victories.

"KOINONIA" CALL LETTERS

Finally, in 1981, we had the approval of government agencies and the Federal Communications Commission gave us the license to begin operation. Construction began immediately on the giant transmitter tower.

We had been earnestly praying about what call letters to request from the Federal Communications Commission. We wanted something that would both embrace the area of the ministry and bring glory to God. The Sunday School class we were attending was called "Koinonia"—a Greek word meaning "rich fellowship in the Spirit." The first three letters of that word also indicated the tri-state area we served: Kentucky, Ohio, and Indiana. That was it! We were granted the license for WKOI-TV, Richmond, Indiana, also serving Dayton and Cincinnati.

—— V ——

"Koinonia" — a Greek word meaning "rich fellowship in the Spirit."

The Lord had, without a shadow of a doubt, directed me to build a Christian television station, but He didn't tell me He wanted me to leave my employment and manage it. In fact, the closer we came to actually broadcasting, the more I felt that someone else might be much better suited for the task.

WHAT A RELIEF!

Several people had told me about a "Praise the

Lord" program that was produced in Southern California, hosted by Paul and Jan Crouch. I had never met them but learned they were expanding their small network of stations. I thought, "If they are already providing Christian programming 24 hours a day, why not let them have the station?"

After making several inquiries, I learned that their organization was called Trinity Broadcasting Network and I phoned their headquarters in Tustin, California.

An efficient, friendly secretary answered the phone.

"May I help you?" she asked.

—— V ——

"Tell him that God has told me to give him a television station in Cincinnati, Ohio."

"Yes," I'd like to speak with Paul Crouch.

The woman replied, "Well, I am sure you understand that he is very busy and probably won't be able to speak to you. Can you leave a message?"

I responded, "Yes. Tell him that God has told me to give him a television station in Cincinnati, Ohio."

It was only a few seconds before Paul Crouch was on the line and his first words were, "Where?"

"Cincinnati," I answered.

A few weeks later we met and signed the station

54

over to TBN. In 1982, Paul and Jan Crouch came to the station and pulled the power switch to begin broadcasting the Gospel on Channel 43.

What a relief! Now I could give total attention to my business endeavors and thank God for allowing us to be a part of launching a marvelous ministry.

I had obeyed the voice of God and felt my days in Christian broadcasting were over.

At least, that's what I thought!

CHAPTER FOUR

RUNNING WITH THE VISION

*Write the vision and make it plan
on tablets, that he may run who reads it.*
– HABAKKUK 2:2

Everything seemed to be right on schedule. For twenty three years I had been in the world of business. My career path was planned and I was tracking my progress carefully. I knew exactly what it would take for me to retire at the age of 55 so that Tina and I could move to sunny Florida. I was even ahead of my projections.

My involvement in building a Christian television station was simply being obedient to God's call. I felt it was only for a certain time and a certain place.

But then my life turned upside down. One night in

1983, the voice of the Lord spoke to me again, saying, "Garth, it's time for a career change. Throw that retirement plan away. I want you to be in full-time service for Me."

UNCHARTED WATERS

At the time, I thought my experience in Christian television would be a wonderful memory, but the Lord had much more in store. He told me, "If you follow My directions, you will look back someday and exclaim, 'What a marvelous thing God has done in my life.'"

The Lord wasn't only speaking to me about a physical move, He was expanding my vision to bring the message of Christ through television to the cities of America—and even around the world.

There were two choices. I could stick to my personal schedule and head for a comfortable retirement; or, I could follow God's call into uncharted waters.

However, I knew it would be impossible to focus on both objectives at once.

Actually, the decision was easy. I said farewell to my business ventures and moved our family to Marion,

Illinois, where, in early 1984, a contract was signed and WDDD-TV became WTCT-27. It would become the home base for what the Lord was impressing us to do.

Without question, God had called me to give my total life to spreading His Word through Christian television.

Leading up to this move, we had both been active in God's army as faithful volunteers. In one year alone Tina put over 50,000 miles on our car doing what was necessary to see God's vision fulfilled. Now He was asking even more.

—— *V* ——

First I heard a voice, then the Lord gave me the vision, and now I was running with it!

First I heard a voice, then the Lord gave me the vision, and now I was running with it!

Only the Beginning

Events happened quickly. After just five months on the air in Marion, we made the decision to broaden our schedule to a full 24 hours a day. Trinity Broadcasting Network brought their mobile equipment from

California and Paul and Jan Crouch helped us throw the symbolic big switch to herald the event.

This was only the beginning. In March, 1985, the next full power total Christian television station signed on in Saginaw, Michigan—WAQP-TV, Channel 49—serving the central part of that state.

Then, in December 1986, TCT launched the "Unifier," a remote television production unit that would allow us to broadcast great concerts and major evangelistic services "live."

Following the opening of our initial stations, TCT entered a "stabilizing" period to be certain the ministry was on a firm financial footing.

The flood-gates of expansion were opened in 1990 and TCT—Total Christian Television—entered a time of significant growth.

In June of that year, we launched WNYB-TV, Channel 49, in Buffalo, New York, serving western New York and southern Ontario, Canada. Three months later we pulled the switch and powered up our new station in Rochester, New York—Channel 59.

A Surge of Growth

The Lord wasn't finished. In February, 1991, two

new broadcasting stations signed on in Michigan: Channel 59 in Jackson, and Channel 69 in Lansing, covering southern Michigan with the Gospel. That same month another 5-million watt total Christian television station came on the air: WINM-TV, Channel 63 in Angola, Indiana, reaching parts of Indiana, Michigan, and Ohio. In June, 1991, we launched Channel 66, covering Ft. Wayne, Indiana.

The growth didn't stop there. The first few months of 1992 were just as exciting. In rapid succession WLXI-TV, Channel 61 and Radiant Life Ministries in Greensboro, North Carolina joined the TCT family. We also launched Channel 54 in Paducah, Kentucky, and WTLJ-TV, bringing the Gospel to Muskegon, Grand Rapids, and all of western Michigan with full-power total Christian television.

"Television you can believe in."

The pact we made with our viewers and supporters was to provide what we call, "Television you can believe in."

As the Lord continued to place doors of opportunities before us, I shudder to think what we would have missed by failing to heed His call.

Now, TCT reaches the world through satellite signals and cable television systems.

A DIVINE PARTNERSHIP

The word God instilled in my heart in 1978 is still at the core of our ministry. He said, *"I myself will search for my sheep and look after them"* (Ezekiel 34:11 NIV).

This promise is with me day and night. It is why I go after a television station the moment God directs me to build one, buy one, or put one on the air.

I am thankful that the Lord and I have a divine partnership: If I do my part, He has promised to do His.

——— *V* ———
If I do my part, He has promised to do His.

Over the years, I have learned not to be overly concerned regarding who watches our programs. I'll let the commercial broadcasters who sell advertising do that. Instead, we focus on putting out a full-time signal, allowing God to do His good work. After all, the viewers are not *my* sheep—they are His. He cares when even one of the flock is lost, broken-hearted, hurting, or hungry. He wants to search and find them.

Only when we reach heaven will Tina and I see

those who have been reached through the ministry —the countless people who have been saved, healed, and whose relationships have been restored. We will shake the hands of men and women who have survived a restless, fearful night because God reached into their homes through the medium of Christian television.

Who is the Lord looking for to accomplish His work? All He requires is an individual who is faithful and will respond to what He asks. This was His directive in the Garden, and it has not changed.

In truth, there is a difference between doing what we are "called" to do and doing what "sounds good." We can start a hundred projects that are valid, honest enterprises. But if they are not what God has called us to, we are simply spinning our wheels.

A POINT OF DECISION

The moment I made a covenant with the Lord to follow Him *regardless of the cost*, a great transformation happened in my life.

When I was in the business world, I felt my future depended on personal decisions and self-made strategies. I was a good example of one who "couldn't see the forest for the trees."

Little did I know that God had a world waiting for me that was far greater than anything I could have imagined. But He had to bring me to a point of decision—a moment that required total commitment.

The word "commit" is a tough one. I have to admit that I wrestled with it for a long period of time. I certainly didn't have any trouble embracing the things that brought me comfort and pleasure. You probably don't either.

However, when it comes to committing your life to God's call—no matter what the cost—many people run and hide. But I have learned that it is futile to be constantly filled anxiety or worry. His dream for our life may require that we go through some valleys, but where He wants to lead us is worth any hardship. As the late Oral Roberts so often said, "God is a good God!"

A LIFE-LONG RESOLUTION

The true test of your love for the Lord is the vow you are willing to make. After everything your heavenly Father has done for you, it doesn't seem too much to ask.

Entering into a marriage, you don't say, "I really love you, but I am not going to make a total commitment. I'll give you my time, even my money, but there are some parts of my life that you can't have"? Or, "I'll live with you the rest of my life if I feel like it, but right now I'm just not sure."

Can you imagine what kind of a marriage relationship that would produce? I'm glad Tina and I have a stronger union. To be honest, we've gone through some trials during our marriage, but it was our life-long vow before God and each other that carried us through.

Trying to find a detour around the road of commitment only prolongs a day of decision that will eventually come. You can run from obligations for only so long, but someday you will face them.

You can run from obligations for only so long, but someday you will face them.

God's Word tells us, *"And as it is appointed for men to die once, but after this the judgment"* (Hebrews 9:27).

If you are truly sincere in your love for the Lord and your relationship with Him, the decision to surrender "all" should not be a difficult one. God desires, deserves, and even more, He demands it. *"For it is written: 'As I live, says the Lord, every knee shall bow to Me, and every tongue shall confess to God"* (Romans 14:11).

GOD'S ORDERS, NOT MINE

Our heavenly Father knows what is best for us and His path is always better than one of our own choosing. To me, there is no question concerning what God wants me to do. But my commitment includes the fact that if He should give me new and different marching orders in the future, I am ready to obey.

If God's assignment for me is to build Christian television stations for the rest of my life, that will be my ministry. If it is for a shorter period of time and God raises up somebody else, I will willingly step aside. One day the Lord may tell me, "Garth, you are released from TCT. The ministry has accomplished everything I wanted it to do through you."

Should that day arrive, I will shout, "Praise the Lord" and follow His leading.

It is a mistake to cling to anything the Lord doesn't

want us to embrace. After all, the ministry God calls us to is not ours—it all belongs to Him.

You Have a Vital Role

I believe the Lord has a specific call on your life. He has a unique place of service for each of us in His Kingdom. Perhaps you have not taken the time to seek His face or to hear His voice, yet He desires to reveal His plan for your future. When He calls, you must be ready to respond, "Lord, I'm yours completely."

——— V ———

Every believer plays a pivotal role in fulfilling the Great Commission.

The longer I am involved in Christian television, the more I realize that every believer plays a pivotal role in fulfilling the Great Commission.

No two individuals are alike. Some have been called to leadership, others to prayer, some to presenting their unique talents, and many to financial support. They are all part of the body of Christ—*equal in the sight of God.*

Please realize that all ministry is God's, and He has called you for service just as much as He has called me. Most important is that we totally dedicate ourselves to what He asks of us.

Never forget: the Lord will not ask you to do anything He has not already prepared you for. I've never known a person who was embarrassed by following God's will.

Over and over again, Tina and I look at the past 30-plus years and with joy, say, "What a marvelous thing He has done."

CHAPTER FIVE

WHO IS CHARTING YOUR COURSE?

*Your word is a lamp to my
feet and a light to my path.*
— PSALM 119:105

'll never forget the advice my grandmother gave me. She said, "You have to look beyond the end of your own nose to find out what the world is all about."

I've come to the conclusion that far too many live their entire lives in a chronic, "near-sighted" condition. It is almost as though their vision reaches as far as the end of their nose, hits a mirror and they say: "There is the answer to all of my needs—it's *me*."

Those who adopt such a view are headed for deep disappointments. God does not intend for us to become self-centered creatures. Instead, He taught us that it is "more blessed to give than to receive," and that we should "love our neighbors as ourselves."

A SERVANT'S HEART

My mother has gone on to be with the Lord, but she lived her life without being overly concerned with her own needs. Her greatest moments of joy were found in simple acts of serving others —whether it was babysitting with great grandchildren or taking a meal to someone who was bedridden.

At times there were those who took advantage of her kindness, but she just smiled and went right on serving.

Did she complain? Never. Did she ask for anything in return? No.

I remember when we would visit her and Tina would say, "Mom, let's go to the beauty shop and get your hair done."

"Oh, that's okay. I can do it myself," she replied.

If we could get her to a shopping center, we would encourage her, "Isn't it time you had a new pair of shoes?"

"No," she laughed, "these are still good. Why don't you get a pair for yourself?"

Mom's love for the Lord ran deep—faithful to the church, faithful in prayer, but never calling attention to herself in the process.

In her declining years she lived in an area where she couldn't see her son on television, but every month she sent a small check to help keep Christian programming beaming into the homes of others.

Her life was a lesson straight out of the New Testament. She taught me a great deal about being a servant rather than a master. This is what the Lord wants of us.

One of the basic spiritual principles is that when we respond to the burden God places on our heart, He will respond by meeting our own needs. But if we remain consumed with our own desires, we become transformed by the forbidden tree in the center of the Garden—and will eventually be destroyed.

She taught me a great deal about being a servant rather than a master.

The Bible makes it crystal clear what happens when we turn our eyes from the promises of God and begin to look at selfish desires.

WHERE IS HE LEADING?

Perhaps you recall what happened to Abram and his nephew Lot. There was strife among each of their herdsmen because the land couldn't support both their livestock when they were grazing together. Abram said to Lot, *"Please let there be no strife between you and me, and between my herdsmen and your herdsmen; for we are brethren. Is not the whole land before you? Please separate from me. If you take the left, then I will go to the right; or, if you go to the right, then I will go to the left"* (Genesis 13:8-9).

Abram generously gave Lot first choice. And what did he choose? *"Lot lifted his eyes and saw all the plain of Jordan, that it was well watered everywhere (before the Lord destroyed Sodom and Gomorrah) like the garden of the Lord, like the land of Egypt as you go toward Zoar"* (Genesis 13:10).

——v——
Sadly, Lot forgot the promises of God and looked for immediate satisfaction.

Sadly, Lot forgot the promises of God and looked for immediate satisfaction. *"Abram dwelt in the land of Canaan, and*

Lot dwelt in the cities of the plain and pitched his tent even as far as Sodom" (Genesis 13:12).

However, Abram stayed right where he was and was blessed beyond measure.

What happened to Lot? We all know the sordid story of Sodom and Gomorrah. Lot's problems began when he turned his head toward that evil city. Even as he and his wife finally fled, God gave the world a powerful lesson. When Lot's wife diverted her focus from what was ahead and looked back, she turned into a pillar of salt.

THE RIGHT PATH

Some of us are guilty of acting like little children. Instead of listening to the voice of the Almighty, we brag, "I can do it by myself." At times we even conclude, "I don't need to bother God. I can do His work for Him."

This was certainly true of Abram's wife, Sarai. She could not bear children, so she thought she would help God out. The Bible records, *"She had an Egyptian maidservant whose name was Hagar. So Sarai said to Abram, 'See now, the Lord has restrained me from bearing children. Please, go in to my maid; perhaps I shall obtain children by her.' And Abram heeded the voice of Sarai"* (Genesis 16:1-2).

Reading those words, I thought, "That is just like so many individuals today. Instead of waiting on God, they are impatient and want to do things their own way."

If you are tempted to follow your own path, refresh your memory with the dramatic story of the Children of Israel. They saw God perform miracle after miracle as they departed from Egypt. God even supplied them with jewels, clothing, and supernatural health. He *"brought them out with silver and gold, And there was none feeble among His tribes"* (Psalm 105:37).

When they reached the sea, however, they made a huge mistake. The army of Egypt was behind them, the sea was ahead of them, yet they took their eyes off the Lord.

Even after God performed a miracle that saved their lives, they still did not learn their lesson. When God provided manna in the desert, they grumbled and complained.

Think of what happened at Mount Sinai. When God's Law was given to Moses, the people were turning to a golden calf for answers. Instead of rejoicing over being led by a "cloud by day and a fire by night," they were looking at a man-made idol. Is it any wonder that they had to endure plagues and suffering?

WHERE ARE YOU LOOKING?

It never pays to become the object of your own attention. The Bible tells us the disastrous consequences that happen when you become the ruler over your life. In the time of the judges, *"there was no king in Israel; everyone did what was right in his own eyes"* (Judges 21:25).

—— *V* ——

It never pays to become the object of your own attention.

Now it came to pass, in the days when the judges ruled, that there was a famine in the land. And a certain man of Bethlehem, Judah, went to sojourn in the country of Moab, he and his wife and his two sons. The name of the man was Elimelech, the name of his wife was Naomi, and the names of his two sons were

Mahlon and Chilion; Ephrathites of Bethlehem, Judah. And they went to the country of Moab and remained there. Then Elimelech, Naomi's husband, died; and she was left, and her two sons" (Ruth 1:1-3).

In the midst of the famine, Elimelech turned his gaze toward Moab—a type of the world. Instead, he should have been looking at Bethlehem, Judah—"the house of bread" and "the house of praise." Because he looked at the world, he perished.

KEEP YOUR EYES ON THE LORD

In Sunday School we learned what happened to powerful Samson. Instead of focusing on the source of his strength, he turned his eyes toward Delilah and lost everything. Throughout human history, the prime objective of Satan is to get people to divert their attention from the One who loves them the most.

People who fail to center their attention on the Lord pay a horrible price. Judas is an example.

During the days leading to Christ's crucifixion, Mary washed His feet with perfume. *"But there were some who were indignant among themselves, and said, 'Why was this fragrant oil wasted? For it might have been sold for more than three hundred denarii and given to the poor.' And they criticized her sharply"* (Mark 14:4-5).

At this event, Judas Iscariot was present. And instead of looking at Christ, he began to think about the value of the perfume and what he considered to be an extravagant waste. Satan took control of Judas' critical nature and he later betrayed the Lord for 30 pieces of silver.

NOT THE STORM, BUT THE SAVIOR

On another occasion, the disciples were almost shipwrecked until Jesus appeared before them, walking on the water. Peter, exercising great faith, began to walk toward Him. Jesus told him, *"'Come.' And when Peter had come down out of the boat, he walked on the water to go to Jesus. But when he saw that the wind was boisterous, he was afraid; and beginning to sink he cried out, saying, 'Lord, save me!'"* (Matthew 14:29-30).

It was only when Peter took his eyes off of the Lord

that he began to be engulfed by the stormy waves.

TURN TOWARD THE VOICE

During the ministry of the disciples, people were transformed by simply looking in a new direction. In Jerusalem, at the temple gate called Beautiful, there was a lame man who had been crippled from birth. He saw Peter and John about to enter the temple and pleaded for alms. *"And fixing his eyes on him, with John, Peter said, 'Look at us.' So he gave them his attention, expecting to receive something from them"* (Acts 3:4-5).

The disciple took the man by the hand and lifted him up.

Peter said, *"Silver and gold I do not have, but what I do have I give you: In the name of Jesus Christ of Nazareth, rise up and walk"* (verse 6).

The disciple took the man by the hand and lifted him up, and immediately *"his feet and ankle bones received strength. So he, leaping up, stood and walked and entered the temple with them; walking, leaping, and praising God"* (Acts 3:7-8).

The cripple was instantly healed because he heard a voice and looked in a new direction.

ARE YOU LISTENING?

The minute we start operating in our own authority instead of God's, we are headed for failure. Long ago I learned that calling on Jesus produced far greater results than calling on myself. There is authority in His holy Name.

Regardless of any situation, you can turn your eyes toward the Lord. In the Book of Acts, when Stephen was being persecuted because of presenting the Gospel to the Sanhedrin, he looked beyond his accusers. *"When they heard these things they were cut to the heart, and they gnashed at him with their teeth. But he, being full of the Holy Spirit, gazed into heaven and said, 'Look! I see the heavens opened and the Son of Man standing at the right hand of God!'"* (Acts 7:54-56)

Why wait for circumstances to force you to look to the Lord? Day by day, hour by hour, make Him the center of your life. He has given each of us a free choice to make our own decisions, but the truly happy man is the one who is listening for God's voice.

Remember the words of the psalmist: *"Blessed is the man Who walks not in the counsel of the ungodly, nor stands in the path of sinners, nor sits in the seat of the scornful; but his delight is in the law of the Lord, and in His law he meditates day and night"* (Psalm 1:1-2).

What are the results of such actions? *"He shall be like a tree planted by the rivers of water, that brings forth its fruit in its season, whose leaf also shall not wither; and whatever he does shall prosper"* (Psalm 1:3).

What an amazing promise!

CHAPTER SIX

SOWING FOR THE HARVEST

*He who sows sparingly will
also reap sparingly, and he who sows
bountifully will also reap bountifully.*
– 2 CORINTHIANS 9:6

In the beginning, God gave the first inhabitants an unusual responsibility. He asked Adam and Eve to both "tame" and "tend" the earth.

The Creator said, *"Let Us make man in Our image, according to Our likeness; let them have dominion over the fish of the sea, over the birds of the air, and over the cattle, over all the earth and over every creeping thing that creeps on the earth"* (Genesis 1:26).

In addition to giving man authority over every creature," He asked that his numbers should increase and that he should "subdue" the land. *"Then God* blessed them, and God said to them, 'Be fruitful and multiply; fill the earth and subdue it; have dominion over the fish of the sea, over the birds of the air, and over every living thing that moves on the earth" (verse 28).

That was an awesome order.

YOUR AUTHORITY

I can imagine Adam's excitement. His assignment was to observe, sort, classify, and give names to all the earth's animals. It was God's way of letting him know, "I am delegating authority and responsibility to you."

—— V ——

"I am delegating authority and responsibility to you."

According to Scripture, *"Out of the ground the Lord God formed every beast of the field and every bird of the air, and brought them to Adam to see what he would call them. And whatever Adam called each living creature, that was its name. So Adam gave names to all cattle, to the birds of the air, and to every beast of the field"* (Genesis 2:19-20).

From Genesis to Revelation, God makes His

82

intentions known. *"You have made him to have dominion over the works of Your hands; You have put all things under his feet, all sheep and oxen; even the beasts of the field, the birds of the air, and the fish of the sea That pass through the paths of the seas"* (Psalm 8:6-8).

Man had been given a divine duty.

TENDER LOVE AND CARE

The Creator gave Adam a second great responsibility. Not only was he to "tame" the earth and its creatures, but he was to "tend" to its needs. *"Then the Lord God took the man and put him in the garden of Eden to tend and keep it"* (Genesis 2:15).

The Almighty knew that what He created would require wise conservation of resources and careful "gardening" to prepare for the future. God makes available what is good for us but He expects us to add some "TLC"—*Tender Love and Care.*

Yes, the Garden was beautiful at creation, but without "custodians" to cultivate it, the weeds would have choked out its splendor.

I once heard about an admiring visitor who said to

a farmer, "You and the Lord have certainly built a beautiful place here."

Smiling, the farmer replied, "You should have seen it when God had it all by Himself!"

A GIFT, NOT A RIGHT

Without a doubt, the Lord expects us to work hand in hand with Him. And there is something else He wants us to tend. He has given us the ability to think and to reason; He desires that we take care of our intellectual resources.

You and I were born totally unique in all creation —with a mind and a spirit. Scripture tells us, *"God created man in His own image; in the image of God He created him"* (Genesis 1:27).

In addition, we have a responsibility to till the soil of our personal and human relationships. If God wanted us to be alone, He would not have decreed that man was to propagate the earth. Eve was not just his wife, but an equal partner—a co-worker with whom to have love and companionship.

Far too often we forget whose world it is. It doesn't belong to us, we are only taking care of it for its rightful owner. For that reason we need to be constantly reminded that our rule is not absolute or independent. We have been given the chance to be a "gardener" in God's Kingdom as a subordinate to the Almighty. It is a gift, not a right.

In the words of Winston Churchill, "The price of greatness is responsibility."

WE ARE STEWARDS

We must never forget that God alone is the Creator of everything in the universe. As Scripture states, *"Every good gift and every perfect gift is from above"* (James 1:17).

Man may adapt, alter, and discover, but he does not create anything.

——— *V* ———

Man may adapt, alter, and discover, but he does not create anything.

God has given us an amazing opportunity. He asks us to be stewards over all we now have—and all we may someday become.

According to His plan, we are the keepers of our emotions, our thoughts, our heart, our will, and even our finances. Whatever the Lord has given, large or small, He asks that you look after it with diligence.

In truth, we only keep what we send ahead to heaven. Everything else is left behind. This is why the Bible tells us, *"Command those who are rich in this present age not to be haughty, nor to trust in uncertain riches but in the living God, who gives us richly all things to enjoy. Let them do good, that they be rich in good works, ready to give, willing to share, storing up for themselves a good foundation for the time to come, that they may lay hold on eternal life"* (1 Timothy 6:17-19).

—— *V* ——
In truth, we only keep what we send ahead to heaven.

FAITHFULNESS AND FINANCES

In a parable, Jesus told the unforgettable story of a man who was unfaithful with the funds God had entrusted to him.

He who is faithful in what is least is faithful also in much; and he who is unjust in what is

86

least is unjust also in much. Therefore if you have not been faithful in the unrighteous mammon, who will commit to your trust the true riches? And if you have not been faithful in what is another man's, who will give you what is your own?

No servant can serve two masters; for either he will hate the one and love the other, or else he will be loyal to the one and despise the other. You cannot serve God and mammon" (Luke 16:10-13).

This is a message we cannot ignore. If we are not trustworthy and faithful with our finances, why should God commit true riches—His mercy, His forgiveness, His peace, and His love?

RECLAIMING SATAN'S TERRITORY

Being a Christian broadcaster, I am painfully aware of what happened when people failed to take dominion over television when it was first discovered. Instead of preaching against "the one-eyed monster" —as it was called from pulpits—the clergy should have seized the opportunity to claim the media for Christ.

In comparison to today's programming, the early days of television were tame—hardly worth getting upset about. The shows were built around family values and wholesome entertainment. There were no "Desperate Housewives" or steamy "Soaps." But slowly, and subtly, the viewpoint changed until it became almost an affront to righteousness.

The devil took advantage of an opportunity when he saw one. Inch by inch the moral standard was slowly lowered until the viewers did not fully comprehend what filth was coming into their living rooms.

We throw up our hands and exclaim, "How did this happen?" God's people complained, but did not aggressively seize the potential.

One of the major reasons I am drawn to Christian television is because I believe we must reclaim Satan's territory.

I do not feel there is anything that can replace the fellowship and teaching of the local church, but I am saddened by the reality that many of the buildings are open only two or three hours each week.

A NEW DAY

Christian television is open 24 hours a day. Plus, it serves a vital need for those who find it totally impossible to attend a local church—the physician won't release them from the hospital, the warden won't unlock the prison gates, or the boss won't let them off on Sunday morning.

—— V ——
Look around and you will see how the nature of evangelism is changing.

Look around and you will see how the nature of evangelism is changing. Door-to-door witnessing has become impossible in many communities. Because of high crime areas, giant apartments with tight security, and a nation that no longer sits on the front porch and waves to neighbors, we are not reaching people in traditional ways.

For many reasons, I believe God is pleased that we are touching men, women, and children who would never darken the door of a church.

Night after night we receive calls from people who are restless and can't sleep. As they turn on our programming, God convicts them of their sin and they call to pray with a Prayer Partner.

I rejoice that one day we will see them in heaven. Why? Because we are taking back what the devil so cleverly tried to steal.

TAKE CHARGE!

The penetration of television can enter almost any door. It is God's creation and I am convinced it is part of His plan to usher in the return of Christ. After the media's perversion by Satan, it was almost too late when Christians finally caught the vision to reclaim it.

Since He gave the medium to us, all He requires is that we take charge and tend to it for His purposes. When we keep our attention on the Master and feel His great burden and compassion for souls, we can understand why it is imperative to "Give the winds a mighty voice: Jesus saves! Jesus saves!"

During a "Praise-A-Thon" or at the times we ask viewers to support our ministry, some can't see the vision because obstacles get in the way.

I remember the day a man called my office and complained, "I would donate to your ministry if you took (so-and-so) off the air. I just don't like his program."

The caller was so obsessed with the one thing he *didn't* like that he failed to appreciate the other 167 hours a week. His attention was misdirected.

A NETWORK OF PRAYER PARTNERS

I still marvel at what takes place behind the scenes at TCT. We now have eight Prayer Centers in the United States and Asia, offering around-the-clock prayer responses to viewer's needs. These are staffed by a network of over 500 Prayer Partners who volunteer their time to personally place the needs of the caller before the Lord.

—— *V* ——
Hundreds of calls are received every day, and the results prove the awesome power of prayer.

Hundreds of calls are received every day, and the results prove the awesome power of prayer. We rejoice at the reports of salvations, answered needs, deliverances, and miracles of healing.

You can reach our Prayer Partners by dialing 800-232-9855.

LESSONS FROM THE WATERS

In recent months there has been an increase in prayer requests from people who are facing economic difficulties. One of our Prayer Partners told me, "You can sense fear in the voices of many who call. They are anxious and concerned about what the future holds."

As I began to think about this, the Lord reminded me of two events that happened several years ago.

The first was when Tina and I were flying out to attend the National Association of Broadcasters convention which is held annually in Las Vegas, Nevada.

As you may know, I have been a pilot for years and TCT makes use of a private plane to visit our stations and other events. This time, after refueling in Albuquerque, we decided to fly along the stunning Grand Canyon, and into Vegas.

After leaving the canyon area, further down the Colorado River was a picturesque sight. About 30 miles from Las Vegas, the blue waters of Lake Mead were glistening in the sun. This is the largest reservoir in the United States—over 110 miles long with a shoreline of 550 miles. It was created in 1936 when the giant Hoover Dam was built.

The second recollection the Lord reminded me of was the time we were flying up to our television station in Buffalo, New York. The air traffic controller directed us over Niagara Falls. Again, it was an awesome spectacle. Steam was rising from where the waters fell 176 feet below, then continued their journey down the Niagara river. They convert the power of the water into electricity.

REMOVE THE BARRIER OF FEAR

As these two scenes were replayed in my mind's eye, the Lord impressed upon me their significance. He was letting me know that Lake Mead represented His blessings, but a giant dam of fear was holding them back— preventing them from flowing.

His blessings and favor are available, but worry and anxiety are blocking their release.

His blessings and favor are available, but worry and anxiety are blocking their release.

Then I heard the Lord speak to my heart, "If people will remove the barrier of fear, My blessings will flow like the Niagara—and will generate tremendous power."

When troubled times arise and you are worried over your health, family, or finances, let God speak to you through His Word. Declare, *"The Lord is my light and my salvation; Whom shall I fear? The Lord is the strength of my life; Of whom shall I be afraid?...*

——*V*——
Let the blessings flow!

Though an army may encamp against me, my heart shall not fear; Though war may rise against me, in this I will be confident" (Psalm 27:1,3).

Remember, *"God has not given us a spirit of fear, but of power and of love and of a sound mind"* (2 Timothy 1:7).

Let the blessings flow!

It's Planting Time

God pours out His favor in many ways, but we must never forget that the law of sowing and reaping established by God has never been abolished or repealed. Before we reap we must learn to sow. As caretakers of His garden, it's a lesson we must continue to learn. *"Do not be deceived, God is not mocked; for whatever a man sows, that he will also reap"* (Galatians 6:7).

The apostle Paul further explains this truth by saying, *"For he who sows to his flesh will of the flesh reap corruption, but he who sows to the Spirit will of the Spirit reap everlasting life. And let us not grow weary while doing good, for in due season we shall reap if we do not lose heart. Therefore, as we have opportunity, let us do good to all, especially to those who are of the household of faith"* (verses 8-10).

The principle has universal application. If a man sows wild oats he will not reap delicious strawberries —he must plant strawberries. If a man scatters seeds to please his fleshly desires, he will surely reap a harvest of spiritual decay and death.

GET READY FOR A HARVEST

It makes sense to plant by using God's instruction book. When you keep His commandments and faithfully look after what He has given, you'll be able to give the testimony of the psalmist: *"He who dwells in the secret place of the Most High Shall abide under the shadow of the Almighty. I will say of the Lord, 'He is my refuge and my fortress; My God, in Him I will trust. Surely He shall deliver you from the snare of the fowler, And from the perilous pestilence. He shall cover you with His feathers, And under His wings you shall take refuge; His truth shall be your shield and buckler'"* (Psalm 91:1-4).

What are you sowing? Where are you planting? By following God's guidance, on the authority of the Word, you will reap a bountiful harvest.

CHAPTER SEVEN

A LIVING TRUST

You will keep in perfect peace him
whose mind is steadfast, because he trusts
in you. Trust in the Lord forever, for
the Lord...is the Rock eternal.

– ISAIAH 26:3-4 NIV

Before I was old enough to remember—when I was only two years old—my father left my mother. It created a painful void in my life. I did not see him again until I was a grown man of thirty.

As you can imagine, I had a hard time understanding a loving relationship between a son and a father. When a minister would preach, "You have a Father in heaven who cares about you," it was difficult for me to comprehend.

I thought "So what? What is a father?" It was someone I didn't know.

In my subconscious, I was not sure I could ever

97

really know God as my Father. There was no meaning-ful experience in my life that I could relate it to. As a result I had a tough time believing that God had a special interest in me.

> *—— V ——*
> *"Did He really care about Garth Coonce? Was the Word of God what it proclaimed to be?"*

I had accepted Christ as my personal Savior and I did not have a problem being a servant in His Kingdom. But when it came to a Father and son relationship, and the idea that He had chosen me, my mind was filled with questions.

I wondered, "Did He really care about Garth Coonce? Was the Word of God what it proclaimed to be?"

ADOPTED INTO HIS FAMILY

Many years later, when I heard His voice and He called me to build a television station I had even more doubts. Why, of all people, would He pick me for such a giant task? I would pray, "Lord, you must be making a mistake. It can't be me. It must be someone else."

Over and over, the Lord would offer words of reassurance, "I have chosen you. You have been adopted into My family. You are My son and I am your Father."

Thankfully, I took the Lord at His word, acted on His leading, and He has never failed me—not one time. As a result, my relationship with my heavenly Father has grown stronger and stronger until today I know what it means to say, *"Trust in the Lord with all your heart, and lean not on your own understanding; in all your ways acknowledge Him, and He shall direct your paths"* (Proverbs 3:5-6).

_____ *V* _____

"I have chosen you. You have been adopted into My family."

"PROVE ME NOW"

On the journey of life, we have two choices. We can either *test* God, or we can *trust* Him.

Let me encourage you to read the words of Malachi regarding what we give to the Lord. You will discover it is more than advice about tithes and offerings. It concerns the matter of trust—and what it means to "prove" that you can take God at His word. *"'Bring all the tithes into the storehouse, that there may be food in My house, and prove me now in this,' says the Lord of hosts, 'If I will not open for you the windows of heaven and pour out for you such blessing that there will not be room enough to receive it'"* (Malachi 3:10).

In The Living Bible it is translated, *"Try it! Let me prove it to you! Your crops will be large, for I will guard them from insects and plagues. Your grapes won't shrivel away before they ripen,' says the Lord Almighty"* (verse 10).

——— *ν* ———

In these trying times, what a promise we have from heaven!

In these trying times, what a promise we have from heaven!

BETTER THAN TESTING

I'm sure you are familiar with the principle: "What we give we will receive." We don't give to test the Lord. Instead, we take Him at His word and offer Him our complete trust.

In real life, this is how it works. If you give trust you

are going to receive trust back. But if you decide to "test" Him, what is going to happen? You can expect to receive a test.

Personally, I certainly don't want to face any more trials. By placing our confidence in the Master and taking care of *His* needs, we will be blessed in the process. *"And my God shall supply all your need according to His riches in glory by Christ Jesus"* (Philippians 4:19).

———*V*———
Many have not learned the importance of knowing where to place their trust.

However, many have not learned the importance of knowing where to place their trust. They lose their direction and continually search for answers in the wrong places.

"KEEP YOUR EYES ON THE BALL"

I still remember the first year my grandson, Tommy, played Little League baseball. When I came to watch his games, he wanted so much to hit the ball out of the park for "Papa."

As the ball came over the plate, he would swing for

all he was worth—so hard that he would spin around like a top and tumble to the ground.

At one game, I called him over and said, "Tommy, it is great that you want to hit a home run, but it's not going to happen until you learn to keep your eyes on the ball. When you are swinging that hard, you just can't see it."

I encouraged him, "The next time you're at bat, try this for me: Watch the ball from the moment it leaves the pitcher's hand until you see it hit the bat. Just try to make contact with the ball and get a base hit. Don't forget. Keep your eye on the ball."

—— *V* ——
"Don't forget. Keep your eye on the ball."

It worked! That was the game he got a base hit and scored the winning run. I think I was more excited than he was. And I know it is a valuable lesson he will be able to apply to many areas of his life.

THE SECRET

Some time back, I used to go fishing with a friend who was a superb "fly" fisherman. He could take a fly rod and throw the hook anywhere he wanted—and the fish would bite.

But when I tried it, the hook would hang up in a tree, or land in a spot I didn't choose. Frustrated, I asked him, "What's your secret?"

His answer was simple. "I just keep my eye on the exact location I want the hook to land. Everything else falls into place."

Winning the Race

This reminds me of three young boys who were playing in the snow. A elderly man walked up and asked, "Would you like to try a new kind of race? I'll give the winner a prize."

Well, the boys quickly agreed and the gentleman told them that his race would be one that required a little skill. "I will go over to the other side of the field," he explained, "and when I give you the signal, you will start to run. The one whose footsteps are the straightest in the snow will be declared the winner."

When the race began, the first boy kept looking at his feet to see if his steps were straight.

The second fellow kept looking at his friends to see

what they were doing.

However, the third boy won the race because his steps were a perfect line in the snow. He didn't look down. He didn't look around. He kept his eyes firmly on the finish line.

"Trust in Me! Don't deviate to the left or to the right."

There is a powerful lesson you can learn from those boys. God is telling us: "Trust in Me! Don't deviate to the left or to the right."

THE LIGHT OF THE WORLD

It's exciting to know that Jesus doesn't make it difficult for us to see Him. He is the light of the world—a beacon set upon a hill. Day by day, we see more clearly as we move closer to the goal.

There's one thing that will guarantee an eternity in heaven: keep your sight firmly fixed on Jesus. We should be *"confident of this very thing, that He who has begun a good work in you will complete it until the day of Jesus Christ"* Philippians 1:6).

Think of how He is "perfecting" us. As we are drawn and move near to Christ, we become more and more like Him so that "on that day" we will be perfect.

THE FAITH FACTOR

Friend, it is not worth the risk of diverting our attention. If we do, we will be-come a weary traveler—falling into ditches, taking the wrong road, and facing Satan's detours. But if we stay on the path He has planned for us, we will reach our divine destination. This is why you must keep your sight firmly fixed on Jesus and allow Him to become your constant point of reference.

—— V ——
Keep your sight firmly fixed on Jesus and allow Him to become your constant point of reference.

When I look back over the years, I can see how the grace of God has worked in my life and the amazing things that have been accomplished for His Kingdom. But looking ahead is another matter. God's plan is that *"we walk by faith, not by sight"* (2 Corinthians 5:7).

To have faith requires absolute trust, but some individuals are skeptical and say, "I'm not ready yet.

First, I am going to test the waters."

Speaking personally, I can tell you that it is far better to jump right in when a "stirring in the waters" happens. By faith, receive everything God has purposed for you.

I love the words of the old song, "Launch out into the deep, Oh let the shoreline go."

DON'T DELAY

When our total reliance is in Christ, something is going to happen that will be as automatic as breathing. By being "near to the heart of God," you will have a passion for the souls of men, women, and young people that you never knew possible. Suddenly, you will feel an all-encompassing burden for the "lost sheep" He spoke of. You will become a partner with Him in the work of redemption.

You will become a partner with Him in the work of redemption.

Millions of people have heard the message, but many have failed to place their trust in the Lord. Some day it will suddenly be too late.

Hear the Word of the Almighty: *"Wisdom calls aloud outside; she raises her voice in the open squares. She cries out in the chief concourses, at the opening of the gates in the city she speaks her words: 'How long, you simple ones, will you love simplicity? For scorners delight in their scorning, and fools hate knowledge. Turn at my reproof; Surely I will pour out my spirit on you; I will make my words known to you"* (Proverbs 1:20-23).

But here is the Lord's warning. *"Because I have called and you refused, I have stretched out my hand and no one regarded, because you disdained all my counsel, and would have none of my reproof, I also will laugh at your calamity; I will mock when your terror comes, when your terror comes like a storm, and your destruction comes like a whirlwind, when distress and anguish come upon you. Then they will call on me, but I will not answer; they will seek me diligently, but they will not find me"* (verses 24-28).

I certainly don't want to find myself in such a predicament!

THERE'S GOOD NEWS

Why procrastinate? There is no better time than right now to establish a "living trust" with the living Lord. You don't want to hear the words, "It's too late."

Unfortunately, many will. *"For you closed your eyes to the facts and did not choose to reverence and trust the Lord...That is why you must eat the bitter fruit of having your own way, and experience the full terrors of the pathway you have chosen"* (Proverbs 1:28,30 The Living Bible).

However, there is good news. The last verse of the chapter tells us, *"But all who listen to me shall live in peace and safety, unafraid"* (verse 33).

Our listening is essential. You will never know God's blessing by testing Him.

- You may need a healing.
- You may be looking for employment.
- You may need your marriage restored.
- You may have a wayward child who needs to be brought back into the fold.

Regardless of the dilemma you face, never challenge the Lord; always trust in Him fully. Take Him at His promise: "Before you even ask, I will answer."

You have a heavenly Father who deeply cares about you. Today, He is asking for your love and trust.

CHAPTER EIGHT

FROM VISION TO VICTORY

*But thanks be to God! He gives us
the victory through our Lord Jesus Christ.*
– 1 CORINTHIANS 15:57 NIV

I t is one thing to hear a voice, and quite another to see the vision.

In the natural, what happens in life when our eyesight becomes impaired? Most people visit an optometrist and receive a prescription for a pair of glasses. The goal is to have 20/20 vision—equal focus in both eyes.

The Word of God contains prescriptions, too. They are found in "20:20" Scriptures that hold the key to our spiritual sight. For example, we are told in 2 Chronicles 20:20 to believe in the Lord. King Jehoshaphat said, *"Hear me, O Judah and you inhabitants of Jerusalem: Believe in the Lord your God, and you shall be established; believe His prophets, and you shall prosper. "*

SEE THE SAVIOR

If you want perfect sight, the answer is easy: believe on Christ. We should also rejoice that He is alive and was seen of men. In John 20:20, after the Resurrection, Jesus told His disciples, *"Peace be unto you.' Now when He had said this, He showed them His hands and His side. Then the disciples were glad when they saw the Lord."*

Christ demonstrated that who was standing before them was truly their risen, victorious Savior. When they realized this they celebrated.

In His Sermon on the Mount, Jesus explained exactly what action to take if we want to have unobstructed vision. Speaking of our condemnation of others, He said, *"And why do you look at the speck in your brother's eye, but do not consider the plank in your own eye? Or how can you say to your brother, 'Let me remove the speck out of your eye'; and look, a plank is in your own eye? Hypocrite! First remove the plank from your own eye, and then you will see clearly to remove the speck out of your brother's eye"* (Matthew 7:3-5).

A MARVELOUS PLAN

Back in the Garden of Eden, God knew that if Adam and Eve ate of the forbidden tree they would be destroyed. He also knew that—as a result of their disobedience—He would have to place a plan of redemption into motion.

In that moment God foresaw what would someday take place. He would be required to send His only Son to die on a cross—made from a tree.

It became the symbol of man's only salvation.

How significant! The tree Adam and Eve focused on, in essence, became the cross on which Christ would hang. It became the symbol of man's only salvation.

When we look to the Lord it guarantees that what God has in store for us will be ours. But He warns, "If you take your eyes off me and look at what is forbidden, you begin carving the cross."

The Father did not desire that man should suffer the agony of sin and death—nor did He wish the same for His Son. But because His first creation turned their attention from the beautiful Garden to the forbidden tree, the world would never be the same.

DON'T CRUCIFY HIM AGAIN

We are admonished to look in the right direction —to the Savior, not to sin and self. When we fail to obey, something takes place that few people ever consider: we crucify Christ once more. He cares for us so much that when we reject Him, He feels the pain and anguish afresh.

We must never allow Christ to suffer again. Remember the high price He paid. *"But God demonstrates His own love toward us, in that while we were still sinners, Christ died for us"* (Romans 5:8).

—— *V* ——
We must never allow Christ to suffer again.

If we yield to temptation and take our eyes off the Lord, we require Christ to return to Calvary's rugged cross.

DON'T BECOME BLINDED

Speaking directly to this issue, the apostle Paul wrote, *"For it is impossible for those who were once enlightened, and have tasted the heavenly gift, and have become partakers of the Holy Spirit, and have tasted the good word of God and the powers of the age to come, if they fall away, to renew them again to repentance, since they crucify again for themselves the Son of God, and put Him to an open shame"* (Hebrews 4-6).

It shouldn't come as a surprise that Satan desires to have us turn our back on the Lord. He delights in seeing Christ return to the Tree again and again.

When the serpent spun his great lie in the Garden, he discussed our vision. Satan said, *"For God knows that in the day you eat of it your eyes will be opened, and you will be like God, knowing good and evil"* (Genesis 3:5). But instead of receiving sight, man became blinded to the things of God.

A NEW VISION

You may question, "What can we do to have our

vision restored?" There is only one answer: we must look to the Son of God. Paul counseled"

> *Therefore we also, since we are surrounded by so great a cloud of witnesses (speaking of all of the great people of faith who are now in heaven), let us lay aside every weight, and the sin which so easily ensnares us, and let us run with endurance the race that is set before us, looking unto Jesus, the author and finisher of our faith, who for the joy that was set before Him endured the cross, despising the shame, and has sat down at the right hand of the throne of God* (Hebrews 12:1-2).

In a nutshell, "Look in the right direction. Look to Jesus." The result of a new vision changes our life dramatically.

Just before Christ ascended to heaven, He promised to send a counselor and a guide—*someone who would lead us in the right direction.* He sent the Holy Spirit.

The Son of God is asking, *"If you love Me, keep My commandments. And I will pray the Father, and He will give you another Helper, that He may abide with you forever, even the Spirit of truth, whom the world cannot receive, because it neither sees Him nor knows Him; but you know Him, for He dwells with you and will be in you"* (John 14:15-17).

Next, the Lord told the disciples, *"A little while longer and the world will see Me no more, but you will see Me. Because I live, you will live also"* (verse 19) The Holy Spirit allows us to see Christ.

The Almighty knew we did not have the power to overcome the advances of Satan without divine help. This is why the Spirit descended.

—— *V* ——

The Holy Spirit allows us to see Christ.

When you ask Him to be your guide, you can *"walk worthy of the calling with which you were called, with all lowliness and gentleness, with longsuffering, bearing with one another in love, endeavoring to keep the unity of the Spirit in the bond of peace. There is one body and one Spirit, just as you were called in one hope of your calling; one Lord, one faith, one baptism"* (Ephesians 4:1-5)

Why try to stumble through the darkness alone when you have the Holy Spirit to empower your vision?

WHAT AN EXCHANGE!

Now for the greatest news of all! The Father's plan makes it possible to share in the rest of God's garden —to enjoy the Fruit of the Spirit. What an exchange! Instead of eating from a tree that would destroy, God has given us a vast new orchard—a brand new vineyard.

Hear what the Lord is saying: "Do you want fruit? I will supply it abundantly."

Yes, it is possible for man to be restored from his error of taking his eyes off of the Almighty. In this new garden, the Spirit delights in filling those who are hungry. He feeds us with the fullness of life which truly satisfies.

In the Word we learn, *"But the fruit of the Spirit is love, joy, peace, longsuffering, kindness, goodness, faithfulness, gentleness, self-control. Against such there is no law. And those who are Christ's have crucified the flesh with its passions and desires. If we live in the Spirit, let us also walk in the Spirit"* (Galatians 5:22-25).

Followers of Christ have nailed their natural desires

to His cross. We celebrate this fact by taking up our cross daily to crucify our carnal cravings. Paul said, *"Instead of asking Christ to return to the cross, I affirm...in Christ Jesus our Lord, I die daily"* (1 Corinthians 15:31).

—— V ——

To enjoy clear vision, follow the footsteps of God's Son.

To enjoy clear vision, follow the footsteps of God's Son. The Holy Spirit will not only help you, He will *sustain* you on your journey.

RETURN TO THE PATH

As part of Satan's attempt to divert us from the paths of righteousness, he places a never-ending stream of distractions in our way. Some are even *good* activities that seem harmless at the start. But if he can cause us to become absorbed in our own interests, we have little time to seek the Lord.

It is imperative that we return to what God intended—to look to His Son, to love one another, and to place our affections on things above. *"Look to Me, and be saved, all you ends of the earth! For I am God, and there is no other"* (Isaiah 45:22).

Since the dawn of creation to this very hour, God continues to send this message of hope: "If you will hear My voice, I will give you a vision and prepare you for a mighty victory."

ON THE BRINK OF A MIRACLE!

I can recall the day several years ago when Satan was trying everything imaginable to destroy the ministry and to discourage Tina and me—in fact I was on the verge of giving up. I cried out to the Lord for an answer.

At the time we were in Saginaw, Michigan, in the middle of a Praise-A-Thon, asking viewers to support the television outreach. The phones were just not ringing. On the third night we were at the point of both frustration and exhaustion when a familiar face walked through the door. It was Mike Adkins.

"Garth, the Lord spoke to me to drive to Saginaw to encourage you," said Mike. "Also, I have just written a new song and would like to share it if you'll allow me to."

Without the slightest hesitation I said, "Yes! Do anything you want!"

Mike began to sing the words: "Don't Give Up On the Brink of a Miracle."

THE FLOODGATES OF BLESSING

Over in a darkened corner of the studio, tears began to fall down my cheeks. I felt that song was just for me! And it must have been for someone else, too. One by one, those telephones began to ring.

Suddenly, people were rejoicing, they were giving their financial support, they were finding Christ!

God knows where we are and exactly what we need. He has a Mike Adkins to send along just at the right time.

—— V ——

I felt that song was just for me!

Instead of being consumed by our problems and looking to ourselves for the answer, we need to get back to basics. The Lord asks that we never give up caring for the things He has given as our responsibility.

When we are faithful, He has a harvest planned that we will not have room to store. Our barns will be full—and running over.

The floodgates of God's blessings continue to this

very day. In 2009, TCT added Channel 47 in Cleveland, Akron, and Canton, Ohio—serving 1.7 million households. This, plus worldwide signals that reach 1.5 billion people lets me know that when God speaks, we must obey. We are part of His purpose to present the Gospel "to every creature."

VICTORY IS YOURS!

From the moment man fell into sin, God began unfolding His plan of redemption. He sent the best thing He had in heaven—His only Son—to be born as a man and to die on a cross. His blood became the covering for our sin. He was buried in a grave, but on the Third Day He rose triumphantly. What a Mighty God we serve!

The Lord ascended into heaven where He sits at the right hand of God, ready to make intercession for those who want to be reconciled with their Maker. If you have never accepted Christ as your Savior, take this moment to pray these words from your heart.

Dear Jesus. I believe that you are the Son of God and that you died on the Cross for me. Forgive me of my sin. Cleanse my heart and

*prepare a place for me in heaven. I thank you
for saving me now.*

God may not ask you to build a television station or
minister in a foreign nation, but He has a unique and
exciting purpose He is waiting to reveal.

Just as the miracle Jesus performed for blind
Bartimaeus of Jericho, He wants to remove the scales
from your eyes and bring you into the brilliance of His
marvelous light.

Are you listening for His voice? Are you prepared
to receive His vision for your future? If so, get ready for
a grand celebration. Victory is yours!

NOTES

_____

_____

_____

_____

_____

_____

_____

_____

_____

_____

_____

_____

_____

_____

_____

_____

_____

_____

_____

_____

_____

_____

To Contact the Author
or to Learn More About TCT:

TCT Ministries
P.O. Box 1010
Marion, IL 62959

Phone: 618-997-9333
U.S. Prayer Center: 313-534-1818
Internet: www.tct.tv
Email: correspondence@tct.tv